Reading
&
Writing

- - - - -

A Personal Account

Reading
&
Writing

- - - - -

A Personal Account

by

V. S. Naipaul

NEW YORK REVIEW BOOKS

New York

THIS IS A NEW YORK REVIEW BOOK
PUBLISHED BY THE NEW YORK REVIEW OF BOOKS

READING AND WRITING: A PERSONAL ACCOUNT
by V. S. Naipaul

This edition published in 2000
in the United States of America by
The New York Review of Books
1755 Broadway
New York, NY 10019
www.nybooks.com

Library of Congress Cataloging-in-Publication Data

Naipaul, V. S. (Vidiadhar Surajprasad), 1932–
    Reading & writing: a personal account / V. S. Naipaul.
        p. cm.
    ISBN 0-940322-38-2 (alk. paper)
        1. Naipaul, V. S. (Vidiadhar Surajprasad), 1932– 2. Naipaul, V. S.
(Vidiadhar Surajprasad), 1932– Books and reading. 3. Naipaul, V. S.
(Vidiadhar Surajprasad), 1932– Authorship. 4. East Indians—
Trinidad—Social life and customs. 5. Authors, Trinidadian—20th
century—Biography. 6. Trinidadians—England—Biography. 7. Books
and reading. 8. Authorship. I. Title: Reading and writing. II. Title.

PR9272.9.N32 Z47 2000
823'.914—dc21
[B]
                                                                99-049615

ISBN 0-940322-38-2

Printed and bound by R. R. Donnelley & Sons
Manufactured in Mexico
February 2000

for David Pryce-Jones

A L S O   B Y

V . S .   N A I P A U L

NONFICTION

Between Father and Son
Beyond Belief
India: A Million Mutinies Now
A Turn in the South
Finding the Center
Among the Believers
The Return of Eva Perón with *The Killings in Trinidad*
India: A Wounded Civilization
The Overcrowded Barracoon
The Loss of El Dorado
An Area of Darkness
The Middle Passage

FICTION

A Way in the World
The Enigma of Arrival
A Bend in the River
Guerrillas
In a Free State
The Mimic Men
A Flag on the Island
Mr. Stone and the Knights Companion
A House for Mr. Biswas
Miguel Street
The Suffrage of Elvira
The Mystic Masseur

Acknowledgment

- - - - -

This essay was written for the Charles Douglas-Home Memorial Trust. Charles Douglas-Home was editor of *The Times of London* from 1982 until his death in 1985, when the trust was set up to award an annual prize in his memory.

Contents

- - - - -

Reading and Writing   *1*

The Writer in India   *4 1*

READING

AND

WRITING

1.

- - - - -

"I have *no memory at all*. That's one of the
great defects of my mind: I keep on brooding
over whatever interests me, by dint of examin-
ing it from different mental points of view I
eventually see something new in it, and I *alter
its whole aspect*. I point and extend the tubes
of my glasses in all ways, or retract them."

— STENDHAL,
The Life of Henry Brulard

I WAS ELEVEN, no more, when the wish came
to me to be a writer; and then very soon it was a
settled ambition. The early age is unusual, but I
don't think extraordinary. I have heard that serious
collectors, of books or pictures, can begin when
they are very young; and recently, in India, I was told
by a distinguished film director, Shyam Benegal,

that he was six when he decided to make a life in cinema as a director.

With me, though, the ambition to be a writer was for many years a kind of sham. I liked to be given a fountain pen and a bottle of Waterman ink and new ruled exercise books (with margins), but I had no wish or need to write anything; and didn't write anything, not even letters: there was no one to write them to. I wasn't especially good at English composition at school; I didn't make up and tell stories at home. And though I liked new books as physical objects, I wasn't much of a reader. I liked a cheap, thick-paged children's book of Aesop's fables that I had been given; I liked a volume of Andersen's tales I had bought for myself with birthday money. But with other books—especially those that schoolboys were supposed to like—I had trouble.

For one or two periods a week at school—this was in the fifth standard—the headmaster, Mr. Worm, would read to us from *Twenty Thousand Leagues Under the Sea*, from the Collins Classics series. The fifth standard was the "exhibition" class and was important to the reputation of the school. The exhibitions, given by the government, were for the island's secondary schools. To win an exhibition was to pay no secondary school fees at all and to get free books right through. It was also to win a kind of fame for oneself and one's school.

I spent two years in the exhibition class; other bright boys had to do the same. In my first year, which was considered a trial year, there were twelve exhibitions for the whole island; the next year there were twenty. Twelve exhibitions or twenty, the school wanted its proper share, and it drove us hard. We sat below a narrow white board on which Mr. Baldwin, one of the teachers (with plastered-down and shiny crinkly hair), had with an awkward hand painted the names of the school's exhibition winners for the previous ten years. And—worrying dignity—our classroom was also Mr. Worm's office. He was an elderly mulatto, short and stout, correct in glasses and a suit, and quite a flogger when he roused himself, taking short, stressed breaths while he flogged, as though he were the sufferer. Sometimes, perhaps just to get away from the noisy little school building, where windows and doors were always open and classes were separated only by half-partitions, he would take us out to the dusty yard to the shade of the saman tree. His chair would be taken out for him, and he sat below the saman as he sat at his big desk in the classroom. We stood around him and tried to be still. He looked down at the little Collins Classic, oddly like a prayer book in his thick hands, and read Jules Verne like a man saying prayers.

Twenty Thousand Leagues Under the Sea wasn't an examination text. It was only Mr. Worm's way of introducing his exhibition class to general reading. It was meant to give us "background" and at the same time to be a break from our exhibition cramming (Jules Verne was one of those writers boys were supposed to like); but those periods were periods of vacancy for us, and not easy to stand or sit through. I understood every word that was spoken, but I followed nothing. This sometimes happened to me in the cinema; but there I always enjoyed the idea of being at the cinema. From Mr. Worm's Jules Verne I took away nothing and, apart from the names of the submarine and its captain, have no memory of what was read for all those hours.

By this time, though, I had begun to have my own idea of what writing was. It was a private idea, and a curiously ennobling one, separate from school and separate from the disordered and disintegrating life of our Hindu extended family. That idea of writing—which was to give me the ambition to be a writer—had built up from the little things my father read to me from time to time.

My father was a self-educated man who had made himself a journalist. He read in his own way. At this time he was in his early thirties, and still learning. He read many books at once, finishing none, looking not for the story or the argument in any book but for the special qualities or character of the writer. That was where he found his pleasure, and he could savor writers only in little bursts.

Sometimes he would call me to listen to two or three or four pages, seldom more, of writing he particularly enjoyed. He read and explained with zest and it was easy for me to like what he liked. In this unlikely way—considering the background: the racially mixed colonial school, the Asian inwardness at home—I had begun to put together an English literary anthology of my own.

These were some of the pieces that were in that anthology before I was twelve: some of the speeches in *Julius Caesar*; scattered pages from the early chapters of *Oliver Twist*, *Nicholas Nickleby*, and *David Copperfield*; the Perseus story from *The Heroes* by Charles Kingsley; some pages from *The Mill on the Floss*; a romantic Malay tale of love and running away and death by Joseph Conrad; one or two of Lamb's *Tales from Shakespeare*; stories by O. Henry and Maupassant; a cynical page or two, about the Ganges and a religious festival, from *Jesting Pilate* by Aldous Huxley; something in the same vein from *Hindoo Holiday* by J. R. Ackerley; some pages by Somerset Maugham.

The Lamb and the Kingsley should have been too old-fashioned and involved for me. But somehow—no doubt because of the enthusiasm of my father—I was able to simplify everything I listened to. In my mind all the pieces (even those from *Julius Caesar*) took on aspects of the fairy tale, became a little like things by Andersen, far off and dateless, easy to play with mentally.

But when I went to the books themselves I found it hard to go beyond what had been read to me. What I already knew was magical; what I tried to read on my own was very far away. The language was too hard; I lost my way in social or historical detail. In the Conrad story the climate and vegetation was like what lay around me, but the Malays seemed extravagant, unreal, and I couldn't place them. When it came to the modern writers their stress on their own personalities shut me out: I couldn't pretend to be Maugham in London or Huxley or Ackerley in India.

I wished to be a writer. But together with the wish there had come the knowledge that the literature that had given me the wish came from another world, far away from our own.

2.

- - - - -

WE WERE AN immigrant Asian community on a small plantation island in the New World. To me India seemed very far away, mythical, but we were at that time, in all the branches of our extended family, only about forty or fifty years out of India. We were still full of the instincts of people of the Gangetic plain, though year by year the colonial life around us was drawing us in. My own presence in Mr. Worm's class was part of that change. No one so young from our family had been to that school. Others were to follow me to the exhibition class, but I was the first.

Mangled bits of old India (very old, the India of nineteenth-century villages, which would have been like the India of earlier centuries) were still with me, not only in the enclosed life of our extended family, but also in what came to us sometimes from our community outside.

One of the first big public things I was taken to was the *Ramlila*, the pageant-play based on the *Ramayana*, the epic about the banishment and later triumph of Rama, the Hindu hero-divinity. It was done in an open field in the middle of sugar cane, on the edge of our small country town. The male performers were barebacked and some carried long bows; they walked in a slow, stylized, rhythmic way, on their toes, and with high, quivering steps; when they made an exit (I am going now by very old memory) they walked down a ramp that had been dug in the earth. The pageant ended with the burning of the big black effigy of the demon king of Lanka. This burning was one of the things people had come for; and the effigy, roughly made, with tar paper on a bamboo frame, had been standing in the open field all the time, as a promise of the conflagration.

Everything in that *Ramlila* had been transported from India in the memories of people. And though as theater it was crude, and there was much that I would have missed in the story, I believe I understood more and felt more than I had done during *The Prince and the Pauper* and *Sixty Glorious Years* at the local cinema. Those were the very first films I had seen, and I had never had an idea what I was watching. Whereas the *Ramlila* had given reality, and a lot of excitement, to what I had known of the *Ramayana*.

The *Ramayana* was the essential Hindu story. It was the more approachable of our two epics, and it lived among us the way epics lived. It had a strong and fast and rich narrative and, even with the divine machinery, the matter was very human. The characters and their motives could always be discussed; the epic was like a moral education for us all. Everyone around me would have known the story at least in outline; some people knew some of the actual verses. I didn't have to be taught it: the story of Rama's unjust banishment to the dangerous forest was like something I had always known.

It lay below the writing I was to get to know later in the city, the Andersen and Aesop I was to read on my own, and the things my father was to read to me.

3.

- - - - -

THE ISLAND WAS small, 1,800 square miles, half a million people, but the population was very mixed and there were many separate worlds.

When my father got a job on the local paper we went to live in the city. It was only twelve miles away, but it was like going to another country. Our little rural Indian world, the disintegrating world of a remembered India, was left behind. I never returned to it; lost touch with the language; never saw another *Ramlila*.

In the city we were in a kind of limbo. There were few Indians there, and no one like us on the street. Though everything was very close, and houses were open to every kind of noise, and no one could really be private in his yard, we continued to live in our old enclosed way, mentally separate from the more colonial, more racially mixed life around us. There were respectable houses with verandas and hanging ferns. But there were also unfenced yards with three or four rotting little two-roomed wooden houses, like the city slave quarters of a hundred years before, and one or two common yard taps. Street life could be raucous: the big American base was just at the end of the street.

To arrive, after three years in the city, at Mr. Worm's exhibition class, cramming hard all the way, learning everything by heart, living with abstractions, having a grasp of very little, was like entering a cinema some time after the film had started and getting only scattered pointers to the story. It was like that for the twelve years I was to stay in the city before going to England. I never ceased to feel a stranger. I saw people of other groups only from the outside; school friendships were left behind at school or in the street. I had no proper understanding of where I was, and really never had the time to find out: all but nineteen months of those twelve years were spent in a blind, driven kind of colonial studying.

Very soon I got to know that there was a further world outside, of which our colonial world was only a shadow. This outer world—England principally, but also the United States and Canada—ruled us in every way. It sent us governors and everything else we lived by: the cheap preserved foods the island had needed since the slave days (smoked herring, salted cod, condensed milk, New Brunswick sardines in oil); the special medicines (Dodd's Kidney Pills, Dr. Sloan's Liniment, the tonic called Six Sixty-Six). It sent us—with a break during a bad year of the war, when we used the dimes and nickels of Canada—the coins of England, from the halfpenny to the half-crown, to which we automatically gave values in our dollars and cents, one cent to a halfpenny, twenty-four cents to a shilling.

It sent us textbooks (Rivington's *Shilling Arithmetic*, Nesfield's *Grammar*) and question papers for the various school certificates. It sent us the films that fed our imaginative life, and *Life* and *Time*. It sent batches of *The Illustrated London News* to Mr. Worm's office. It sent us the Everyman's Library and Penguin Books and the Collins Classics. It sent us everything. It had given Mr. Worm Jules Verne. And, through my father, it had given me my private anthology of literature.

The books themselves I couldn't enter on my own. I didn't have the imaginative key. Such social knowledge as I had—a faint remembered village India and a mixed colonial world seen from the outside—didn't help with the literature of the metropolis. I was two worlds away.

I couldn't get on with English public-school stories (I remember the curiously titled *Sparrow in Search of Expulsion*, just arrived from England for Mr. Worm's little library). And later, when I was at the secondary school (I won my exhibition), I had the same trouble with the thrillers or adventure stories in the school library, the Buchan, the Sapper, the Sabatini, the Sax Rohmer, all given the pre-war dignity of leather binding, with the school crest stamped in gold on the front cover. I couldn't see the point of these artificial excitements, or the point of detective novels (a lot of reading, with a certain amount of misdirection, for a little bit of a puzzle). And when, not knowing much about new reputations, I tried plain English novels from the public library, too many questions got in the way—about the reality of the people, the artificiality of the narrative method, the purpose of the whole set-up thing, the end reward for me.

My private anthology, and my father's teaching, had given me a high idea of writing. And though I had started from a quite different corner, and was years away from understanding why I felt as I did, my attitude (as I was to discover) was like that of Joseph Conrad, himself at the time a just-published author, when he was sent the novel of a friend. The novel was clearly one of much plot; Conrad saw it not as a revelation of human hearts but as a fabrication of "events which properly speaking are *accidents* only." "All the charm, all the truth," he wrote

to the friend, "are thrown away by the . . . mecha-
nism (so to speak) of the story which makes it
appear false."

For Conrad, as for the narrator of *Under
Western Eyes*, the discovery of every tale was a
moral one. It was for me, too, without my knowing
it. It was where the *Ramayana* and Aesop and
Andersen and my private anthology (even the
Maupassant and the O. Henry) had led me. When
Conrad met H. G. Wells, who thought him too
wordy, not giving the story straight, Conrad said,
"My dear Wells, what is this *Love and Mr.
Lewisham* about? What is all this about Jane
Austen? What is it all *about*?"

That was how I had felt in my secondary school,
and for many years afterward as well; but it had not
occurred to me to say so. I wouldn't have felt I had
the right. I didn't feel competent as a reader until I
was twenty-five. I had by that time spent seven
years in England, four of them at Oxford, and I had
a little of the social knowledge that was necessary

for an understanding of English and European fiction. I had also made myself a writer, and was able, therefore, to see writing from the other side. Until then I had read blindly, without judgment, not really knowing how made-up stories were to be assessed.

Certain undeniable things, though, had been added to my anthology during my time at the secondary school. The closest to me were my father's stories about the life of our community. I loved them as writing, as well as for the labor I had seen going into their making. They also anchored me in the world; without them I would have known nothing of our ancestry. And, through the enthusiasm of one teacher, there were three literary experiences in the sixth form: *Tartuffe*, which was like a frightening fairy tale, *Cyrano de Bergerac*, which could call up the profoundest kind of emotion, and *Lazarillo de Tormes*, the mid-sixteenth-century Spanish picaresque story, the first of its kind, brisk and ironical, which took me into a world like the one I knew.

That was all. That was the stock of my reading at the end of my island education. I couldn't truly call myself a reader. I had never had the capacity to lose myself in a book; like my father, I could read only in little bits. My school essays weren't exceptional; they were only crammer's work. In spite of my father's example with his stories I hadn't begun to think in any concrete way about what I might write. Yet I continued to think of myself as a writer.

It was now less a true ambition than a form of self-esteem, a dream of release, an idea of nobility. My life, and the life of our section of our extended family, had always been unsettled. My father, though not an orphan, had been a kind of waif since his childhood; and we had always been half dependent. As a journalist my father was poorly paid, and for some years we had been quite wretched, with no proper place to live. At school I was a bright boy; on the street, where we still held ourselves apart, I felt ashamed at our condition. Even after that bad time had passed, and we had moved, I was eaten up with anxiety. It was the emotion I felt I had always known.

4.

- - - - -

THE COLONIAL GOVERNMENT gave
four scholarships a year to Higher School Certi-
ficate students who were at the top of their group—
languages, modern studies, science, mathematics.
The question papers were sent out from England,
and the students' scripts were sent back there to
be marked. The scholarships were generous. They
were meant to give a man or woman a profession.
The scholarship winner could go at the government's expense to any university or place of higher
education in the British Empire; and his scholarship
could run for seven years. When I won my scholarship—after a labor that still hurts to think about: it
was what all the years of cramming were meant to
lead to—I decided only to go to Oxford and do the
three-year English course. I didn't do this for the
sake of Oxford and the English course; I knew little
enough about either. I did it mainly to get away to

the bigger world and give myself time to live up to my fantasy and become a writer.

To be a writer was to be a writer of novels and stories. That was how the ambition had come to me, through my anthology and my father's example, and that was where it had stayed. It was strange that I hadn't questioned this idea, since I had no taste for novels, hadn't felt the impulse (which children are said to feel) to make up stories, and nearly all my imaginative life during the long cramming years had been in the cinema, and not in books. Sometimes when I thought of the writing blankness inside me I felt nervous; and then—it was like a belief in magic—I told myself that when the time came there would be no blankness and the books would get written.

At Oxford now, on that hard-earned scholarship, the time should have come. But the blankness was still there; and the very idea of fiction and the novel was continuing to puzzle me. A novel was something made up; that was almost its definition. At the same time it was expected to be true, to be drawn from life; so that part of the point of a novel came from half rejecting the fiction, or looking through it to a reality.

Later, when I had begun to identify my material and had begun to be a writer, working more or less intuitively, this ambiguity ceased to worry me. In 1955, the year of this breakthrough, I was able to understand Evelyn Waugh's definition of fiction (in the dedication to *Officers and Gentlemen*, published that year) as "experience totally transformed"; I wouldn't have understood or believed the words the year before.

More than forty years later, when I was reading Tolstoy's Sebastopol sketches for the first time, I was reminded of that early writing happiness of mine when I began to see a way ahead. I thought that in those sketches I could see the young Tolstoy moving, as if out of need, to the discovery of fiction: starting as a careful descriptive writer (a Russian counterpart of William Howard Russell, the *Times* correspondent, not much older, on the other side), and then, as though seeing an easier and a better way of dealing with the horrors of the Sebastopol siege, doing a simple fiction, setting characters in motion, and bringing the reality closer.

A discovery like that was to come to me, but not at Oxford. No magic happened in my three years there, or in the fourth that the Colonial Office allowed me. I continued to fret over the idea of fiction as something made up. How far could the making up (Conrad's "accidents") go? What was the logic and what was the value? I was led down many byways. I felt my writing personality as something grotesquely fluid. It gave me no pleasure to sit down at a table and pretend to write; I felt self-conscious and false.

If I had had even a little money, or the prospects of a fair job, it would have been easy then to let the writing idea drop. I saw it now only as a fantasy born out of childhood worry and ignorance, and it had become a burden. But there was no money. I had to hold on to the idea.

I was nearly destitute—I had perhaps six pounds

—when I left Oxford and went to London to set up as a writer. All that remained of my scholarship, which seemed now to have been prodigally squandered, was the return fare home. For five months I was given shelter in a dark Paddington basement by an older cousin, a respecter of my ambition, himself very poor, studying law and working in a cigarette factory.

Nothing happened with my writing during those five months; nothing happened for five months afterward. And then one day, deep in my almost fixed depression, I began to see what my material might be: the city street from whose mixed life we had held aloof, and the country life before that, with the ways and manners of a remembered India. It seemed easy and obvious when it had been found; but it had taken me four years to see it. Almost at the same time came the language, the tone, the voice for that material. It was as if voice and matter and form were part of one another.

Part of the voice was my father's, from his stories of the country life of our community. Part of it was from the anonymous *Lazarillo*, from mid-sixteenth-century Spain. (In my second year at Oxford I had written to E. V. Rieu, editor of the Penguin Classics, offering to translate *Lazarillo*. He had replied very civilly, in his own hand, saying it would be a difficult book to do, and he didn't think it was a classic. I had nonetheless, during my blankness, as a substitute for writing, done a full translation.) The mixed voice fitted. It was not absolutely my own when it came to me, but I was not uneasy with it. It was, in fact, the writing voice which I had worked hard to find. Soon it was familiar, the voice in my head. I could tell when it was right and when it was going off the rails.

To get started as a writer, I had had to go back to the beginning, and pick my way back—forgetting Oxford and London—to those early literary experiences, some of them not shared by anybody else, which had given me my own view of what lay about me.

5.

- - - - -

IN MY FANTASY of being a writer there had
been no idea how I might actually go about writing
a book. I suppose—I couldn't be sure—that there
was a vague notion in the fantasy that once I had
done the first the others would follow.

I found it wasn't like that. The material didn't
permit it. In those early days every new book meant
facing the old blankness again and going back to
the beginning. The later books came like the first,
driven only by the wish to do a book, with an intu-
itive or innocent or desperate grasping at ideas and
material without fully understanding where they
might lead. Knowledge came with the writing. Each
book took me to deeper understanding and deeper
feeling, and that led to a different way of writing.
Every book was a stage in a process of finding out;
it couldn't be repeated. My material—my past, separated from me by place as well—was fixed and,

like childhood itself, complete; it couldn't be added to. This way of writing consumed it. Within five years I had come to an end. My writing imagination was like a chalk-scrawled blackboard, wiped clean in stages, and at the end blank again, tabula rasa.

Fiction had taken me as far as it could go. There were certain things it couldn't deal with. It couldn't deal with my years in England; there was no social depth to the experience; it seemed more a matter for autobiography. And it couldn't deal with my growing knowledge of the wider world. Fiction, by its nature, functioning best within certain fixed social boundaries, seemed to be pushing me back to worlds— like the island world, or the world of my childhood —smaller than the one I inhabited. Fiction, which had once liberated me and enlightened me, now seemed to be pushing me toward being simpler than I really was. For some years—three, perhaps four— I didn't know how to move; I was quite lost.

Nearly all my adult life had been spent in countries where I was a stranger. I couldn't as a writer go beyond that experience. To be true to that experience I had to write about people in that kind of position. I found ways of doing so; but I never ceased to feel it as a constraint. If I had had to depend only on the novel I would probably have soon found myself without the means of going on, though I had trained myself in prose narrative and was full of curiosity about the world and people.

But there were other forms that met my need. Accident had fairly early on brought me a commission to travel in the former slave colonies of the Caribbean and the old Spanish Main. I had accepted for the sake of the travel; I hadn't thought much about the form.

I had an idea that the travel book was a glamorous interlude in the life of a serious writer. But the writers I had had in mind—and there could have been no others—were metropolitan people, Huxley, Lawrence, Waugh. I was not like them. They wrote at a time of empire; whatever their character at home, they inevitably in their travel became semi-imperial, using the accidents of travel to define their metropolitan personalities against a foreign background.

My travel was not like that. I was a colonial traveling in New World plantation colonies which were like the one I had grown up in. To look, as a visitor, at other semiderelict communities in despoiled land, in the great romantic setting of the New World, was to see, as from a distance, what one's own community might have looked like. It was to be taken out of oneself and one's immediate circumstances—the material of fiction—and to have a new vision of what one had been born into, and to have an intimation of a sequence of historical events going far back.

I had trouble with the form. I didn't know how to travel for a book. I traveled as though I was on holiday, and then floundered, looking for the narrative. I had trouble with the "I" of the travel writer; I thought that as traveler and narrator he was in unchallenged command and had to make big judgments.

For all its faults, the book, like the fiction books that had gone before, was for me an extension of knowledge and feeling. It wouldn't have been possible for me to unlearn what I had learned. Fiction, the exploration of one's immediate circumstances, had taken me a lot of the way. Travel had taken me further.

6.

- - - - -

IT WAS ACCIDENT again that set me to doing another kind of nonfiction book. A publisher in the United States was doing a series for travelers, and asked me to do something about the colony. I thought it would be a simple labor: a little local history, some personal memories, some word pictures.

I had thought, with a strange kind of innocence, that in our world all knowledge was available, that all history was stored somewhere and could be retrieved according to need. I found now that there was no local history to consult. There were only a few guidebooks in which certain legends were repeated. The colony had not been important; its past had disappeared. In some of the guidebooks the humorous point was made that the colony was a place where nothing of note had happened since Sir Walter Raleigh's visit in 1595.

I had to go to the records. There were the reports of travelers. There were the British official papers. In the British Museum there were very many big volumes of copies of relevant Spanish records, dug up by the British government from the Spanish archives in the 1890s, at the time of the British Guiana–Venezuela border dispute. I looked in the records for people and their stories. It was the best way of organizing the material, and it was the only way I knew to write. But it was hard work, picking through the papers, and using details from five or six or more documents to write a paragraph of narrative. The book which I had thought I would do in a few months took two hard years.

The records took me back almost to the discovery. They showed me the aboriginal peoples, masters of sea and river, busy about their own affairs, possessing all the skills they had needed in past centuries, but helpless before the newcomers, and ground down over the next two hundred years to nonentity, alcoholism, missionary reserves, and extinction. In this manmade wilderness then, in the late eighteenth century, the slave plantations were laid out, and the straight lines of the new Spanish town.

At school, in the history class, slavery was only a word. One day in the schoolyard, in Mr. Worm's class, when there was some talk of the subject, I remember trying to give meaning to the word: looking up to the hills to the north of the city and thinking that those hills would once have been looked upon by people who were not free. The idea was too painful to hold on to.

The documents now, many years after that moment in the schoolyard, made that time of slavery real. They gave me glimpses of the life of the plantations. One plantation would have been very near the school; a street not far away still carried the Anglicized French name of the eighteenth-century owner. In the documents I went—and very often—to the city jail, where the principal business of the French jailer and his slave assistant was the punishing of slaves (the charges depended on the punishment given, and the planters paid), and where there were special hot cells, just below the roof shingles, for slaves who were thought to be sorcerers.

From the records of an unusual murder trial—one slave had killed another at a wake for a free woman of color—I got an idea of the slave life of the streets in the 1790s, and understood that the kind of street we had lived on, and the kind of street life I had studied from a distance, were close to the streets and life of a hundred and fifty years before. That idea, of a history or an ancestry for the city street, was new to me. What I had known had seemed to me ordinary, unplanned, just there, with nothing like a past. But the past was there: in the schoolyard, in Mr. Worm's class, below the saman tree, we stood perhaps on the site of Dominique

Dert's Bel-Air estate, where in 1803 the slave *commandeur*, the estate driver or headman, out of a twisted love for his master, had tried to poison the other slaves.

More haunting than this was the thought of the vanished aborigines, on whose land and among whose spirits we all lived. The country town where I was born, and where in a clearing in the sugar cane I had seen our *Ramlila*, had an aboriginal name. One day in the British Museum I discovered—in a letter of 1625 from the king of Spain to the local governor—that it was the name of a troublesome small tribe of just over a thousand. In 1617 they had acted as river guides for English raiders. Eight years later—Spain had a long memory—the Spanish governor had assembled enough men to inflict some unspecified collective punishment on the tribe; and their name had disappeared from the records.

This was more than a fact about the aborigines. It to some extent altered my own past. I could no longer think of the *Ramlila* I had seen as a child as occurring at the very beginning of things. I had imaginatively to make room for people of another kind on the *Ramlila* ground. Fiction by itself would not have taken me to this larger comprehension.

I didn't do a book like that again, working from documents alone. But the technique I had acquired —of looking through a multiplicity of impressions to a central human narrative—was something I took to the books of travel (or, more properly, inquiry) that I did over the next thirty years. So, as my world widened, beyond the immediate personal circumstances that bred fiction, and as my comprehension widened, the literary forms I practiced flowed together and supported one another; and I couldn't say that one form was higher than another. The form depended on the material; the books were all part of the same process of understanding. It was what the writing career—at first only a child's fantasy, and then a more desperate wish to write stories—had committed me to.

The novel was an imported form. For the metropolitan writer it was only one aspect of self-knowledge. About it was a mass of other learning, other imaginative forms, other disciplines. For me, in the beginning, it was my all. Unlike the metropolitan writer I had no knowledge of a past. The past of our community ended, for most of us, with our grandfathers; beyond that we could not see. And the plantation colony, as the humorous guidebooks said, was a place where almost nothing had happened. So the fiction one did, about one's immediate circumstances, hung in a void, without a context, without the larger self-knowledge that was always implied in a metropolitan novel.

As a child trying to read, I had felt that two worlds separated me from the books that were offered to me at school and in the libraries: the childhood world of our remembered India, and the more colonial world of our city. I had thought that the difficulties had to do with the social and emotional disturbances of my childhood—that feeling of having entered the cinema long after the film had started—and that the difficulties would blow away as I got older. What I didn't know, even after I had written my early books of fiction, concerned only with story and people and getting to the end and mounting the jokes well, was that those two spheres of darkness had become my subject. Fiction, working its mysteries, by indirections finding directions out, had led me to my subject. But it couldn't take me all the way.

THE WRITER
AND INDIA

1.

- - - - -

INDIA WAS THE greater hurt. It was a subject country. It was also the place from whose very
great poverty our grandfathers had had to run away
in the late nineteenth century. The two Indias were
separate. The political India, of the freedom movement, had its great names. The other, more personal India was quite hidden; it vanished when memories faded. It wasn't an India we could read about.
It wasn't Kipling's India, or E. M. Forster's, or Somerset Maugham's; and it was far from the somewhat
stylish India of Nehru and Tagore. (There was an
Indian writer, Premchand [1880–1936], whose stories in Hindi and Urdu would have made our Indian
village past real to us. But we didn't know about
him; we were not reading people in that way.)

It was to this personal India, and not the India of independence and its great names, that I went when the time came. I was full of nerves. But nothing had prepared me for the dereliction I saw. No other country I knew had so many layers of wretchedness, and few countries were as populous. I felt I was in a continent where, separate from the rest of the world, a mysterious calamity had occurred. Yet what was so overwhelming to me, so much in the foreground, was not to be found in the modern-day writing I knew, Indian or English. In one Kipling story an Indian famine was a background to an English romance; but generally in both English and Indian writing the extraordinary distress of India, when acknowledged, was like something given, eternal, something to be read only as background. And there were, as always, those who thought they could find a special spiritual quality in the special Indian distress.

It was only in Gandhi's autobiography, *The Story of My Experiments with Truth*, in the chapters dealing with his discovery in the 1890s of the wretchedness of the unprotected Indian laborers in South Africa, that I found—obliquely, and not for long—a rawness of hurt that was like my own in India.

I wrote a book, after having given up the idea. But I couldn't let go of the hurt. It took time—much writing, in many moods—to see beyond the dereliction. It took time to break through the bias and the fantasies of Indian political ideas about the Indian past. The independence struggle, the movement against the British, had obscured the calamities of India before the British. Evidence of those calamities lay on every side. But the independence movement was like religion; it didn't see what it didn't want to see.

For more than six hundred years after 1000 AD the Muslim invaders had ravaged the subcontinent at will. They had established kingdoms and empires and fought with one another. They had obliterated the temples of the local religions in the north; they had penetrated deep into the south and desecrated temples there.

For twentieth-century Indian nationalism those centuries of defeat were awkward. So history was re-jigged; ruler and ruled before the British, conqueror and subject, believer and infidel, became one. In the face of the great British power, it made a kind of sense. Still, to promote the idea of the wholeness of India before the British, it was easier for nationalist writers to go very far back, to pre-Islamic days, to the fifth and seventh centuries, when India was for some the center of the world, and Chinese Buddhist scholars came as pilgrims to Buddhist centers of learning in India.

The fourteenth-century Moroccan Muslim theologian and world traveler Ibn Battuta didn't fit in so easily with this idea of Indian wholeness. Ibn Battuta wished to travel to all the countries of the Muslim world. Everywhere he went he lived on the bounty of Muslim rulers, and he offered pure Arab piety in return.

He came to India as to a conquered Muslim land. He was granted the revenues (or crops) of five villages, then—in spite of a famine—two more; and he stayed for seven years. In the end, though, he had to run. The Muslim ruler in Delhi, Ibn Battuta's ultimate patron, liked blood, daily executions (and torture) on the threshold of his hall of audience, with the bodies left lying for three days. Even Ibn Battuta, though used to the ways of Muslim despots the world over, began to take fright. When four guards were set to watch him he thought his time had come. He had been pestering the ruler and his officials for this and that, and complaining that the ruler's gifts were being soaked up by officials before they got to him. Now, with the inspiration of terror, he declared himself a penitent who had renounced the world. He did a full five-day fast, reading the Koran right through every day of his fast; and when he next appeared before the ruler he was dressed like a mendicant. The renunciation of the theologian touched the hard heart of the ruler, reminded him of higher things, and Ibn Battuta was allowed to go.

In Ibn Battuta's narrative the local people were only obliquely seen. They were serfs in the villages (the property of the ruler, part of the bounty that could be offered the traveler) or simple slaves (Ibn Battuta liked traveling with slave girls). The beliefs of these people had a quaint side but were otherwise of no interest to a Muslim theologian; in Delhi their idols had been literally overthrown. The land had ceased to belong to the local people, and it had no sacredness for the foreign ruler.

In Ibn Battuta it was possible to see the beginnings of the great dereliction of India. To seventeenth-century European travelers like Thomas Roe and Bernier the general wretchedness of the people—living in huts just outside the Mogul palaces—mocked the pretentiousness of the rulers. And for William Howard Russell, reporting in 1858 and 1859 on the Indian Mutiny for *The Times*, and traveling slowly from Calcutta to the Punjab, the land was everywhere in old ruin, with the half-starved ("hollow-thighed") common people, blindly going about their menial work, serving the British as they had served every previous ruler.

Even if I had not found words for it, I had believed as a child in the wholeness of India. The

Ramlila—the pageant play based on the *Ramayana* that we saw performed in an open field just outside our little town—and our religious rites and all our private ways were part of that wholeness; it was something we had left behind. This new idea of the past, coming to me over the years, unraveled that romance, showed me that our ancestral civilization —to which we had paid tribute in so many ways in our far-off colony, and had thought of as ancient and unbroken—had been as helpless before the Muslim invaders as the Mexicans and Peruvians were before the Spaniards; had been half destroyed.

2.

- - - -

FOR EVERY KIND of experience there is a proper form, and I do not see what kind of novel I could have written about India. Fiction works best in a confined moral and cultural area, where the rules are generally known; and in that confined area it deals best with things—emotions, impulses, moral anxieties—that would be unseizable or incomplete in other literary forms.

The experience I had had was particular to me. To do a novel about it, it would have been necessary to create someone like myself, someone of my ancestry and background, and to work out some business which would have taken this person to India. It would have been necessary more or less to duplicate the original experience, and it would have added nothing. Tolstoy used fiction to bring the siege of Sebastopol closer, to give it an added reality. I feel that if I had attempted a novel about India, and mounted all that apparatus of invention, I would have been falsifying precious experience. The value of the experience lay in its particularity. I had to render it as faithfully as I could.

The metropolitan novel, so attractive, so apparently easy to imitate, comes with metropolitan assumptions about society: the availability of a wider learning, an idea of history, a concern with self-knowledge. Where those assumptions are wrong, where the wider learning is missing or imperfect, I am not sure whether the novel can offer more than the externals of things. The Japanese imported the novel form and added it to their own rich literary and historical traditions; there was no mismatch. But where, as in India, the past has been torn away, and history is unknown or unknowable or denied, I don't know whether the borrowed form of the novel can deliver more than a partial truth, a dim lighted window in a general darkness.

Forty to fifty years ago, when Indian writers were not so well considered, the writer R. K. Narayan was a comfort and example to those of us (I include my father and myself) who wished to write. Narayan wrote in English about Indian life. This is actually a difficult thing to do, and Narayan solved the problems by appearing to ignore them. He wrote lightly, directly, with little social explanation. His English was so personal and easy, so without English social associations, that there was no feeling of oddity; he always appeared to be writing from within his culture.

He wrote about people in a small town in South India: small people, big talk, small doings. That was where he began; that was where he was fifty years later. To some extent that reflected Narayan's own life. He never moved far from his origins. When I met him in London in 1961—he had been traveling, and was about to go back to India—he told me he needed to be back home, to do his walks (with an umbrella for the sun) and to be among his characters.

He truly possessed his world. It was complete and always there, waiting for him; and it was far enough away from the center of things for outside disturbances to die down before they could get to it. Even the independence movement, in the heated 1930s and 1940s, was far away, and the British presence was marked mainly by the names of buildings and places. This was an India that appeared to mock the vainglorious and went on in its own way.

Dynasties rose and fell. Palaces and mansions appeared and disappeared. The entire country went down under the fire and sword of the invader, and was washed clean when Sarayu [the local river] overflowed its bounds. But it always had its rebirth and growth.

In this view (from one of the more mystical of Narayan's books) the fire and sword of defeat are like abstractions. There is no true suffering, and rebirth is almost magical. These small people of Narayan's books, earning petty sums from petty jobs, and comforted and ruled by ritual, seem oddly insulated from history. They seem to have been breathed into being; and on examination they don't appear to have an ancestry. They have only a father and perhaps a grandfather; they cannot reach back further into the past. They go to ancient temples; but they do not have the confidence of those ancient builders; they themselves can build nothing that will last.

But the land is sacred, and it has a past. A

character in that same mystical novel is granted a simple vision of that Indian past, and it comes in simple tableaux. The first is from the *Ramayana* (about 1000 BC); the second is of the Buddha, from the sixth century BC; the third is of the ninth-century philosopher Shankaracharya; the fourth is of the arrival a thousand years later of the British, ending with Mr. Shilling, the local bank manager.

What the tableaux leave out are the centuries of the Muslim invasions and Muslim rule. Narayan spent part of his childhood in the state of Mysore. Mysore had a Hindu maharajah. The British put him on the throne after they had defeated the Muslim ruler. The maharajah was of an illustrious family; his ancestors had been satraps of the last great Hindu kingdom of the south. That kingdom was defeated by the Muslims in 1565, and its enormous capital city (with the accumulated human talent that had sustained it) almost totally destroyed, leaving a land so impoverished, so nearly without creative human resource, that it is hard now to see how a great empire could have arisen on that spot.

The terrible ruins of the capital—still speaking four centuries later of loot and hate and blood and Hindu defeat, a whole world destroyed—were perhaps a day's journey from Mysore City.

Narayan's world is not, after all, as rooted and complete as it appears. His small people dream simply of what they think has gone before, but they are without personal ancestry; there is a great blank in their past. Their lives are small, as they have to be: this smallness is what has been allowed to come up in the ruins, with the simple new structures of British colonial order (school, road, bank, courts). In Narayan's books, when the history is known, there is less the life of a wise and enduring Hindu India than a celebration of the redeeming British peace.

So in India the borrowed form of the English or European novel, even when it has learned to deal well with the externals of things, can sometimes miss their terrible essence. I too, as a writer of fiction, barely understanding my world—our family background, our migration, the curious half-remembered

India in which we continued to live for a generation, Mr. Worm's school, my father's literary ambition—I too could begin only with the externals of things. To do more, as I soon had to, since I had no idea or illusion of a complete world waiting for me somewhere, I had to find other ways.

3.

- - - - -

FOR SIXTY OR seventy years in the nineteenth century the novel in Europe, developing very fast in the hands of a relay of masters, became an extraordinary tool. It did what no other literary form—essay, poem, drama, history—could do. It gave industrial or industrializing or modern society a very clear idea of itself. It showed with immediacy what hadn't been shown before; and it altered vision. Certain things in the form could be modified or played with later, but the pattern of the modern novel had been set, and its program laid out.

All of us who have come after have been derivative. We can never be the first again. We might bring new material from far away, but the program we are following has been laid out for us. We cannot be the writing equivalent of Robinson Crusoe on his island, letting off "the first gun that had been fired there since the creation of the world." That (to stay with the metaphor) is the gunshot we hear when we turn to the originators. They are the first; they didn't know it when they began, but then (like Machiavelli in his *Discourses* and Montaigne in his *Essays*) they do know, and they are full of excitement at the discovery. That excitement comes over to us, and there is an unrepeatable energy in the writing.

The long passage below is from the beginning of *Nicholas Nickleby* (1838). Dickens is twenty-six and at his freshest. The material is commonplace. That is its point. Dickens appears to have just discovered (after Boz and Pickwick and *Oliver Twist*) that everything he sees in London is his to write about, and that plot can wait.

> Mr Nickleby closed an account-book which lay on his desk, and, throwing himself back in his chair, gazed with an air of abstraction through the dirty window. Some London houses have a melancholy little plot of ground behind them, usually fenced in by four high whitewashed walls, and frowned upon by stacks of chimneys: in which there withers on, from year to year, a crippled tree, that makes a show of putting forth a few leaves late in autumn when other trees shed theirs, and, drooping in the effort, lingers on, all crackled and smoke-dried, till the following season. . . . People sometimes call these dark yards "gardens"; it is not supposed that they were ever planted, but rather that they are pieces of unreclaimed land, with the withered vegetation of the original brick-field. No man thinks

of walking in this desolate place, or of turning it to any account. A few hampers, half a dozen broken bottles, and such-like rubbish, may be thrown there, when the tenant first moves in, but nothing more; and there they remain until he goes away again: the damp straw taking just as long to smoulder as it thinks proper: and mingling with the scanty box, and stunted everbrowns, and broken flower-pots, that are scattered mournfully about—a prey to "blacks" and dirt.

It was into a place of this kind that Mr Ralph Nickleby gazed.... He had fixed his eyes upon a distorted fir-tree, planted by some former tenant in a tub that had once been green, and left there, years before, to rot away piecemeal.... At length, his eyes wandered to a little dirty window on the left, through which the face of the clerk was dimly visible; that worthy chancing to look up, he beckoned him to attend.

It is delightful, detail by detail, and we can stay with it because we feel, with the writer, that it hasn't been done before. This also means that it can't be done with the same effect again. It will lose its air of discovery, which is its virtue. Writing has always to be new; every talent is always burning itself out. Twenty-one years later, in *A Tale of Two Cities* (1859), in the wine cask scene, the Dickensian hard stare has become technique, impressive but rhetorical, the detail oddly manufactured, the product more of mind and habit than of eye.

> A large cask of wine had been dropped and broken . . . and it lay on the stones just outside the door of the wine-shop, shattered like a walnut-shell.
>
> All the people within reach had suspended their business, or their idleness, to run to the spot and drink the wine. The rough, irregular stones of the street, pointing every way, and designed, one might have thought, expressly to lame all living creatures that approached them,

had dammed it into little pools; these were sur-
rounded, each by its own jostling group or
crowd, according to its size. Some men kneeled
down, made scoops of their two hands joined,
and sipped, or tried to help women, who bent
over their shoulders, to sip, before the wine
had all run out between their fingers. Others,
men and women, dipped in the puddles with
little mugs of mutilated earthenware, or even
with handkerchiefs from women's heads, which
were squeezed dry into infants' mouths. . . .

Only the shattered walnut and the mutilated mug
are like the younger Dickens. The other details will
not create revolutionary Paris (of seventy years
before); they are building up more into the sym-
bolism of the political cartoon.

Literature is the sum of its discoveries. What is
derivative can be impressive and intelligent. It can
give pleasure and it will have its season, short or
long. But we will always want to go back to the

originators. What matters in the end in literature, what is always there, is the truly good. And—though played-out forms can throw up miraculous sports like *The Importance of Being Earnest* or *Decline and Fall*—what is good is always what is new, in both form and content. What is good forgets whatever models it might have had, and is unexpected; we have to catch it on the wing. Writing of this quality cannot be taught in a writing course.

Literature, like all living art, is always on the move. It is part of its life that its dominant form should constantly change. No literary form—the Shakespeare play, the epic poem, the Restoration comedy, the essay, the work of history—can continue for very long at the same pitch of inspiration. If every creative talent is always burning itself out, every literary form is always getting to the end of what it can do.

The new novel gave nineteenth-century Europe a certain kind of news. The late twentieth century, surfeited with news, culturally far more confused, threatening again to be as full of tribal or folk movement as during the centuries of the Roman Empire, needs another kind of interpretation. But the novel, still (in spite of appearances) mimicking the program of the nineteenth-century originators, still feeding off the vision they created, can subtly distort the unaccommodating new reality. As a form it is now commonplace enough, and limited enough, to be teachable. It encourages a multitude of little narcissisms, from near and far; they stand in for originality and give the form an illusion of life. It is a vanity of the age (and of commercial promotion) that the novel continues to be literature's final and highest expression.

Here I have to go back to the beginning. It was out of the colonial small change of the great nineteenth-century achievement that—perhaps through a teacher or a friend—the desire to be a writer came to my father in the late 1920s. He did become a writer, though not in the way he wanted. He did good work; his stories gave our community a past that would otherwise have been lost. But there was a mismatch between the ambition, coming from outside, from another culture, and our community, which had no living literary tradition; and my father's hard-won stories have found very few readers among the people they were about.

He passed on the writing ambition to me; and I, growing up in another age, have managed to see that ambition through almost to the end. But I remember how hard it was for me as a child to read serious books; two spheres of darkness separated me from them. Nearly all my imaginative life was in the cinema. Everything there was far away, but at the same time everything in that curious operatic world was accessible. It was a truly universal art. I don't think I overstate when I say that without the Hollywood of the 1930s and 1940s I would have been spiritually quite destitute. That cannot be shut out of this account of reading and writing. And I have to wonder now whether the talent that once went into imaginative literature didn't in this century go into the first fifty years of the glorious cinema.

ABOUT THE TYPE

The text type, Sabon, was designed by the son of a letter-painter, Jan Tschichold (1902–1974), who was jointly commissioned in 1960, by Monotype, Linotype, and Stempel, to create a typeface which would produce consistent results when produced by hand-setting, or with either the Monotype or Linotype machines.

The German book designer and typographer is known for producing a wide range of designs. Tschichold's early work, considered to have revolutionized modern typography, was influenced by the avant-garde Bauhaus and characterized by bold asymmetrical sans serif faces. With his Sabon design, Tschichold demonstrates his later return to more formal and traditional typography. Sabon is based upon the roman Garamond face of Konrad Berner, who married the widow of printer Jacques Sabon. The italic Sabon is modeled after the work of Garamond's contemporary, Robert Granjon.

In Sabon, Tschichold's appreciation of classical letters melds with the practicality of consistency and readability into a sophisticated and adaptable typeface.

Sabon is a registered trademark of
Linotype-Hell AG and/or its subsidiaries

Interior Design by
Red Canoe, Deer Lodge, TN
Caroline Kavanagh
Deb Koch